ONLINE GAMING
12 THINGS YOU NEED TO KNOW

by Jill Roesler

12 STORY LIBRARY

www.12StoryLibrary.com

12-Story Library is an imprint of Peterson Publishing Company and Press Room Editions.

Produced for 12-Story Library by Red Line Editorial

Photographs ©: dem10/iStockphoto, cover, 1, 12; John Minchillo/Invision for Activision/ AP Images, 4; Huntstock/Thinkstock, 5; Jack Hollingsworth/Digital Vision/Thinkstock, 6; KennyK/Shutterstock Images, 7; Monkey Business Images/Shutterstock Images, 8; Ingram Publishing/Thinkstock, 9; Yuri Arcurs/iStockphoto, 10; Przemek Tokar/Shutterstock Images, 11, 29; Katy Winn/Invision/AP Images, 13; tmcphotos/Shutterstock Images, 14, 28; Dragon Images/Shutterstock Images, 15; Jakub Zak/Shutterstock Images, 16; Syda Productions/ Shutterstock Images, 17; Bloomua/Shutterstock Images, 19; Sergey Sukhorukov/ Shutterstock Images, 18; Sanzhar Murzin/Shutterstock Images, 20; Fuse/Thinkstock, 21; Giulio Fornasar/Shutterstock Images, 22; Konstantin Sutyagin/Shutterstock Images, 23; Barone Firenze/Shutterstock Images, 24; Atelier Sommerland/Shutterstock Images, 25; Stefano Tinti/Shutterstock Images, 27

ISBN
978-1-63235-222-4 (hardcover)
978-1-63235-248-4 (paperback)
978-1-62143-273-9 (hosted ebook)

Library of Congress Control Number: 2015934326

Printed in the United States of America
Mankato, MN
October, 2015

Go beyond the book. Get free, up-to-date content on this topic at 12StoryLibrary.com.

TABLE OF CONTENTS

WHAT IS ONLINE GAMING?

You have just entered Containment Corner in chapter 13 of the online game *Skylanders: Trap Team*. Skylands' most-wanted villains have escaped from Cloudcracker Prison. Your character is a Tech Trap Master. Together with the other Skylanders, you must trap the villains. The Mabu has given you a "villain quest" for Wolfgang, an undead monster. You easily capture Wolfgang and continue the quest.

When a game requires an Internet connection, it is an online game. Online games are played on computers and game consoles. They are even played on mobile devices, such as smartphones and tablets.

Skylanders: Trap Team toys interact with the online game.

You can play online games alone or with a friend.

Gamers play some online games as single players. Or, they can play multiplayer games with friends. Millions of players from all over the world can play in a single game at the same time. This makes online games appealing to many players.

Many gamers enjoy playing offline video games. Online gaming, however, is much more popular. Computers and consoles are used most for online gaming. But mobile gaming is rising in popularity.

2
Average number of gamers per US household in 2014.

- An online game is played over a computer network.
- You can play with people all over the world in multiplayer online games.
- Gaming on mobile phones and tablets is rising in popularity.

HOW DO I STAY SAFE WHILE GAMING?

Before you start online gaming, it's good to know how to keep yourself safe while you play. First, make sure your computer, console, or mobile device is protected. Install protection, such as anti-virus and anti-spyware software. Computer viruses harm your device. Some allow other people to see your personal information. Ask a trusted adult to help you protect your device.

Most online games require you to create an account. Manage your gaming account with safety in mind. Choose a username that does not give away your identity. Never use your actual name as your username. Instead, use a name inspired by something you like, such as "Bookworm100" or "SoccerStar1." Keeping your real name private helps protect your identity online and in real life.

Then, make a strong password for your account. Strong passwords are at least eight characters long. A character is a number, uppercase or lowercase letter, or symbol. Use a combination of characters in your password. Do not write your password down. Create something that only you and a parent can remember.

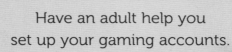

Have an adult help you set up your gaming accounts.

Many accounts give you the chance to include an image. Instead of a photo of yourself, use an avatar. An avatar lets you create your own "virtual self." Just like your username, your avatar can be inspired by something you like to do.

It is important to think about safety when you are playing online. Many games allow you to interact with other players.

Your avatar represents you in an online game.

Some games allow players to chat by text or by voice. Only use voice chat if the game allows you to disguise your voice. If your game does not have that function, use chat instead. If someone sends you a link for a free download, do not open it. It could contain a virus or spyware. Avoid using a webcam when playing an online game. Keeping your real-life identity private helps you stay safe.

Never meet an online stranger in person. If another gamer asks to meet, tell a trusted adult right away. An adult can usually tell if a situation is safe or not. If another player makes you feel uncomfortable, speak up. An adult will know what to do.

6

Months that should pass before you change your password.

- Make sure your computer, console, or mobile device has a firewall and anti-virus and anti-spyware protection before playing online games.
- Never use your actual name as your username.
- If a game does not let you disguise your voice, do not use voice chat online.

WHAT IS CONSOLE GAMING?

A video game console connects to a TV. The players use game controllers to interact with the game. Gamers also can use other accessories, such as joysticks, gamepads, and steering wheels. They make gameplay easier and more enjoyable.

online. Consoles, such as Xbox One, Wii U, and PlayStation 4, do not need to be connected to the Internet. But some features, such as downloading new characters, require an Internet connection. Players might choose to play offline because they do not have an Internet connection.

Video games can be played offline and

Console games require a controller.

2002

Year Microsoft launched Xbox Live, a network that made modern, online console gaming possible.

- Some console games can be played online and offline.
- Gamers can purchase physical copies of games or digital ones through a console's online store.
- You can choose to play games solo or with others.

Others may enjoy playing solo instead of alongside millions of other players.

However, many console games are designed to play online. Consoles connect to the Internet just like a computer. They use the same Internet network. An Internet connection allows players to play with gamers throughout the world.

Console games require you to buy each individual game you play. You can buy a physical copy of the game. It looks like a DVD. Or, you can buy a digital copy through the console's online store. However, it is possible that digital copies will not transfer to future consoles. Examples of console games that can be played by others online include *Minecraft* and *Just Dance 2015*.

Arcade machines are large and heavy.

ARCADE GAMES

In the United States, only a few arcades still exist. Arcades are places where people go to play video games. Each game is played on its own large machine. Today, few young people spend time in arcades playing games such as *Street Fighter 2* on a 500-pound (227-kg) machine. Instead, they play a similar game on a 5-ounce (142-g) smartphone.

9

WHAT IS PC GAMING?

Players who prefer online computer gaming, or PC gaming, use a computer to play online games. According to experts, most online players prefer PC gaming to console gaming. Computers have more power and produce better graphics. Games tend to run more smoothly on computers. Better graphics make games seem realistic. Many PC game creators try to make games look as real as possible.

Some PC games are more difficult to play than others. Real-time strategy (RTS) games are played live with other players. All players take turns together in an RTS game. This makes the game complicated to play. The action moves quickly. Imagine an enemy mothership is

PC games are often more realistic than console games.

RTS players compete against each other in tournaments.

attacking your spaceship in the RTS game *Homeworld Remastered*. If you do not react quickly, your ship could explode. It is difficult to avoid an attack.

PC gamers can buy a month-to-month subscription for some games, such as *Wizard101*. A subscription gives players access to all of the game's content. Free-to-play games let players try a game for free. But often, players must purchase upgrades to access advanced features.

65

Percent of gamers who voted for Steam, a digital game store, as the "Best Resource for PC Games" in 2014.

- PC games tend to have better graphics than console games.
- Real-time strategy games are played live.
- Free-to-play games allow gamers to try a game before buying it.

THINK ABOUT IT

Do you think you would enjoy playing online games on a console or a computer? How would interacting with other players change your gaming experience? List at least three examples.

WHAT ARE THE DIFFERENT TYPES OF ONLINE GAMES?

Gamers have a choice of playing video games designed for either a single player or multiple players. A single-player video game allows players to play alone rather than with others online. Online games are usually multiplayer. They are designed for gamers to play with others over the Internet. Millions of players can play the same game simultaneously in a massively

multiplayer online game (MMO). Some MMOs include voice chat. That way, players can speak to one another while playing.

One type of MMO is a role-playing game (MMORPG). Here, millions of

Some MMO players use voice chat to communicate.

30
Years since the first *The Legend of Zelda* adventure game launched in 1986.

- There are numerous types of online games, including MMOs, MMORPGs, adventure games, shooters, and simulation games.
- In MMOs, millions of gamers play simultaneously.
- Simulation games let players create cities or civilizations, dance, or play sports.

people play together in a single game, just like a regular MMO. The difference is that players create their own characters. Characters start with few skills. The goal of an MMORPG is to grow your character and build its skills. This is called leveling. Many MMORPGs, such as *Wizard101,* take place in a fantasy world. Others, such as *Roblox*, are set in space in the future.

MMOs are not the only type of online game. Adventure games let players discover their own virtual world. Players solve puzzles and collect valuable items on their way through the game. Two popular adventure games are *The Legend of Zelda* and *Disney Infinity: Marvel Super Heroes*. In a shooter game, the player's goal is to shoot objects. Players face enemies or obstacles. Simulation games allow players to have real-world experiences through their gaming systems. Players perform a physical task on screen, but not in real life. Some games allow players to build cities or entire civilizations. In others, players dance or play sports.

EARLY VIDEO GAMES

In 1984, Nintendo released a game called *Duck Hunt. Duck Hunt* was the first of its kind. To win, players used an accessory called a Zapper. The player aimed the gun at the TV screen to shoot at the ducks in the game. In 2014, Nintendo revived the game. *Duck Hunt* can now be played on the Wii U.

WHO PLAYS ONLINE GAMES?

A lot of people think teenage boys play the most video games. But this is a stereotype some people have about gamers. A 2014 study found 48 percent of gamers are women, while 52 percent are men. There are nearly as many female gamers as there are male gamers.

Another study found adult women play more video games than teenage boys do. Mobile devices have increased the number of female players. Women prefer playing online games on their mobile devices. Some people think women prefer playing games such as *Candy Crush Saga*, *Kim Kardashian: Hollywood*, and *Words with Friends*. That is another stereotype. Different female players enjoy different games. Many women enjoy playing brain teaser games and card games on their mobile devices. Others like

Female gamers enjoy playing all types of games.

playing adventure and other games on their computers.

The online games men prefer follow more of a pattern. Males tend to like games full of competition and 3-D navigation. They like games with multiplayer functions so they can play with friends. Experts say many males learn best by doing hands-on activities. That may be why action and adventure games appeal to men and boys the most. But be careful not to stereotype men. Not all men like the same types of games.

Not all male gamers like to play PC or console games.

39

Percent of gamers who are 36 years old or older, the most gamers in any age group.

ESRB

The Entertainment Software Rating Board, or ESRB, rates video games. It has rated more than 21,000 video games in the past 20 years. The ratings are "early childhood," "everyone," "everyone 10+," "teen", "mature," and "adults only." You can use ESRB ratings to find games that are appropriate for you.

- There are many stereotypes about video gamers.
- The number of female gamers is almost equal to the number of male gamers.
- ESRB ratings help you find games that are appropriate for your age.

WHAT ARE THE DANGERS OF ONLINE GAMING?

Online gaming can be fun. However, as you play, remember to look out for potential real-life dangers. When you play games online, the information is stored in your computer or console. Over time, you add more and more personal information to online profiles and gaming websites. This information is collected and used to create your online identity.

If a gaming website or network, such as Xbox Live, asks you to create a profile, do not add personal information. That includes your last name, address, telephone number, or your school. Keeping this information private helps you stay safe. Your online identity can reveal personal information. And future employers, colleges, and coworkers might use

Don't share too much information when you set up your gaming accounts.

your identity to learn more about you.

Never use any of your parent's personal information online, either. That includes using a credit card to make online purchases. If you

Ask adults for permission to use their credit cards.

5

Percent of children between the ages of 5 and 10 who know how to use their parents' credit cards online.

- Gaming is fun, but you need to keep in mind some of the dangers you may face.
- The information you add about yourself online can give away personal details to people who may try to harm you.
- If you download a game or cheat code from an untrusted website, it could contain a virus.

download a game or a "cheat code" from an untrusted website, criminals could try to access the credit card number. Some untrusted games and cheat codes even contain computer viruses. Before you add any of your parent's or your own personal information to a website, ask.

ARE VIOLENT GAMES BAD FOR YOU?

Not all video games are violent. But some online games contain graphic violence. Scientists have studied video game violence. And some people believe violent video games may cause players to become violent in real life. But so far, scientists are unable to say for sure if this is the case.

One study found it takes gamers four minutes to get rid of violent thoughts after playing a violent game. It takes up to ten minutes for their heart rates to return to normal. Some research suggests that violent video games make players less understanding of others' feelings.

Other scientists disagree. Some research suggests violent video games give players a way to release their own anger. A 2007 study found 62 percent of boys played video games to relax. Another 45 percent said games helped them let out angry feelings.

More research suggests violent video games can teach players there are consequences for their actions. Interactions in video games may

Scientists study to learn if video games cause players to become violent.

teach players how to interact in the real world. Sometimes, online characters act violently and get away with it. Most of the time, though, there is a gameplay consequence for violence. Of course, the player is not punished in real life. But the game does help a player to see what kind of consequences there *could* be in real life.

Some gamers think violent games help them let out anger.

THE LEGEND OF ZELDA

The Legend of Zelda contains fantasy violence. But it still teaches valuable lessons. For example, one part of the game is Zelda's Money Making Game. When you gamble in this game, you will either lose 10 rupees or earn 50 rupees. But sometimes you will lose 40 rupees. Gambling in *The Legend of Zelda* teaches the consequences of gambling in the real world.

48.8

Percent of seventh and eighth graders who reported the use of at least one mature-rated video game in a 2010 study.

- Some scientists believe violent games make players more aggressive in real life.
- Others believe violent video games help players release their anger.
- Violent video games can help players learn the consequences of their actions.

IS ONLINE GAMING ADDICTIVE?

Online gaming is different from playing video games offline. Many online games do not have a beginning, middle, and end. This is especially true of MMO games. Because many online games never actually end, some people have trouble turning the game off. Some people use the online gaming community as a way to socialize.

Instead of socializing at school, at parties, or during sports games, they talk to other players in the game.

According to experts, an online gaming addiction is similar to gambling. There are several ways a video game addiction can be destructive. Gaming may get in the way of homework, hygiene, and friends. Using online games to

Some players become addicted to video games.

THINK ABOUT IT

If you play online games, what could make a game addictive? If someone you know became addicted to video games, would you try to stop the addiction?

3

Number of days in a row a man in Taiwan played video games without sleep and with very little to eat.

- Online gaming addictions are similar to gambling addictions.
- Because MMO games never really end, some gamers have trouble turning the game off and being active in the real world.
- A gaming addiction is usually a sign of a deeper problem.

escape social situations is common for addicts.

Players who show signs of addiction are usually experiencing different, deeper problems. For example, they may be the targets of bullying. They might be experiencing trouble at home. If you fear that you or a friend is addicted to video games, seek the help of a trusted adult.

Spend time with friends in real life, not just in online games.

WHAT ARE THE BENEFITS OF ONLINE GAMES?

While some gamers could be addicted to video games, others can benefit greatly from playing. Online games bring people together. While they do not always bring them together physically, they do socially. Online games allow players to talk to one another from across the room, or across the globe.

Cooperative games can help build friendships. A friend who plays with you in a game may be able to help you in the real world, too. Some gamers learn to type and speak other languages by talking to people

Playing games with friends is often more fun than playing alone.

around the world. They teach other gamers about their culture. Many friendships are created online.

Some research suggests gaming may be good for your brain. It may help your ability to reason and remember things. Games may even help you read maps more easily or find your way in an unfamiliar place.

Action and adventure games let players learn about and discover new places. Online puzzle games help players feel more confident. They exercise players' brains, too. Beating a game can give a player a sense of accomplishment.

Games can be played with others across the globe.

70

Minimum percentage of gamers who often play with a friend.

- Cooperative games can help build friendships.
- Games can build a player's teamwork skills.
- Many players get a sense of accomplishment from beating a video game.

HOW DO GAME MAKERS KEEP PLAYERS COMING BACK?

A video game developer's job is to find out what keeps *all* gamers coming back. The term "gameplay" refers to how a player interacts with a game. Many games have a plot, characters, a setting, a climax, and specific challenges. Gameplay connects your character to all of those features.

The replay value of a game determines if players will return to a game more than one time. Some

TREADMILLS

A treadmill is a feature inside a video game. It takes players through the same action more than once to collect some type of object. The gamer might shoot at monsters or throw pies to earn points. The gamer may turn in the points to purchase tools to help the player through the rest of the game.

Game companies host conventions to show off their latest games.

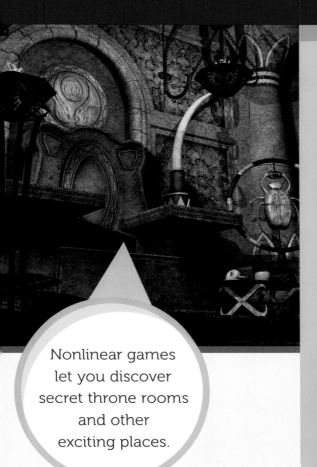

Nonlinear games let you discover secret throne rooms and other exciting places.

$13 billion

Estimated revenue for all MMO games worldwide by 2017.

- Gameplay refers to a character's connection to the plot, setting, other characters, and climax of a video game's story.
- Linear gameplay follows a specific story line, while nonlinear gameplay does not.
- Many role-playing games have nonlinear gameplay with many smaller side quests.

games follow a story, such as the game *Nancy Drew*. The characters start at the beginning, move through the middle, and finally reach the end of the game. This is called linear gameplay. In role-playing games, there are hundreds of side quests and thousands of non-player characters. Many role-playing games have nonlinear gameplay. The game does not follow a story line like a linear game does. Players have more choice in how they spend their time in the game.

According to experts, gamers like to complete side quests more than they like to play the actual game. Many players prefer games that have nonlinear gameplay aspects. Nonlinear games give players more freedom in the game. They do not need to follow a particular story line. They get to decide what their character does.

WHAT IS THE FUTURE OF ONLINE GAMING?

Technology changes things quickly. This includes online video games. Five years ago, gamers were not playing the same types of games they play today. Five years from now, gaming will probably look different.

The gaming community itself has changed. In the past, only those who were truly dedicated to online gaming played. With the popularity of mobile devices today, everyone has an opportunity to play. In fact, gamers do not even have to buy

consoles. They can download video game apps onto their smartphones. An app is considerably cheaper than buying an online game for a console.

Gaming apps are inexpensive and easy to use. They can be installed on multiple devices. Apps often offer

102.7 million

Number of Nintendo Wii, PlayStation 4, and Xbox 360 consoles sold in North America by July 2015.

- Online games five years from now will be quite different from today's games.
- Mobile devices have made gaming popular with all sorts of players.
- Apps make games more affordable and easy to play.

THINK ABOUT IT

What do you think the future of gaming holds? Do you think people will use apps more than consoles and PCs? Why or why not?

26

the same games that online marketplaces, such as Steam or Xbox Live Marketplace, do. Games on apps are similar to the arcade games or side quests in a PC or console game. Gaming on mobile devices is expected to become even more popular.

Educational video games are already used in some classrooms. Research suggests students become more engaged when video games are included in school lessons. They can be used to improve students' problem solving and critical thinking skills. They also help them learn about science, math, and history.

Virtual reality may become common in the games of the future.

No matter how gamers play, game developers will continue to search for new and exciting game features. One is virtual reality. Users wear a headset with a computer. The computer creates a realistic, virtual world the user can see and hear. In 2015, virtual reality technology was not yet ready for gaming. But in the future, it may become as common as a game controller. There are many predictions for the future of online gaming. But no one can know for sure what the next great game will be.

FACT SHEET

- The average gamer is 34 years old. According to the Entertainment Software Association, those gamers have been playing online games for about 14 years. Most gamers enjoy the social aspects of gaming most.

- Casual and social games take the top spot for most-played online games. Online puzzles, board games, and trivia games come in second place. Action, sports, and role-playing games are the third most popular games to play.

- Online games are not just for kids, teens, and young adults. People of all ages enjoy gaming. Even celebrities, including Mila Kunis, Dave Chappelle, and Vin Diesel, enjoy playing online games.

- If your parents play video games, you are more likely to play too. More than one-third of US parents play video games. Ninety-three percent of these parents' children are also gamers.

- The Nintendo Game Boy was the first popular handheld game. The Game Boy came out in 1989. Nintendo made many improvements to the Game Boy over the years. The Game Boy Color came out in 1998, and the Game Boy Advance came out in 2001. In 2011, the Nintendo 3DS took the place of the Game Boy.

GLOSSARY

addiction
The harmful and strong need to have or do something, such as video gaming.

avatar
A figure that represents a particular person in video games.

cooperative
A feature in a video game that allows players to work together as teammates against one or more opponents.

online identity
An identity an Internet user creates by using websites and participating in online communities.

online profile
A social media user's information that is viewable by other users.

personal information
Facts about yourself, such as your age, gender, and grade.

stereotype
To believe unfairly that all people or things with a particular characteristic are the same.

virus
A computer code that causes some unexpected and usually harmful effect.

FOR MORE INFORMATION

Books

Culp, Jennifer. *Online Gaming Safety and Privacy.* New York: Rosen Central, 2014.

Harbour, Jonathan S. *Video Game Programming for Kids.* Boston: Cengage Learning, 2014.

Parkin, Simon. *An Illustrated History of 151 Video Games.* London: Lorenz, 2014.

Websites

ESRB: Ratings Guide
www.esrb.org/ratings/ratings_guide.jsp

NS Teens: Games
www.nsteens.org/Games

TeensHealth: Are Video Games Good for the Mind?
www.kidshealth.org/teen/expert/school_jobs/gaming.html

INDEX

About the Author

Jill Roesler was a professional journalist before she began writing children's books. She enjoys doing research and writing about historical topics as well as modern-day society. Jill is from Minnesota.

READ MORE FROM 12-STORY LIBRARY

Every 12-Story Library book is available in many formats, including Amazon Kindle and Apple iBooks. For more information, visit your device's store or 12StoryLibrary.com.